MW01612092

Copyright © 2018 by William R. & Lona R. Love

All rights reserved. No part of this book may be reproduced or
transmitted in any form or by any means, electronic or mechanical,
including photocopying, recording or by any information storage and
retrieval system without permission in writing from the publisher.

Scriptures taken from the HOLY BIBLE, NEW LIVING TRANSLATION,
Copyright © 1996, 2004, 2007 by Tynsdale House Foundation.
Used by permission of Tynsdale House Publishers, Inc.,
Carol Stream, Illinois 60188. All rights reserved.

E.R. Violet Publishing, LLC
West Des Moines, IA 50266
violetpublish@gmail.com

Printed in the United States of America

Illustrations by Bill Love

Book Design by WORDART, LLC West Des Moines, IA

PastorPickle.com

# This book belongs to

_____

( A child of God )

Lessons for Living Series

# Pastor Pickle
## and the
## Full Box
## of
## Crayons

## Bill & Lona Love

**Kip Kuyper sat alone on the still swing** at the Pioneer Park playground, his head bowed and his cheeks flushed bright red. Pastor Percy Pickle and his dog Doogie, on their daily exercise walk, cautiously approached the swing set.

"Well good Sunday afternoon, Kip Kuyper!" Pastor Pickle called to the boy he recognized from church.

Kip Kuyper looked up and waved to Pastor Pickle, who could tell by the look on Kip Kuyper's face that something was bothering him.

"It's a beautiful afternoon, isn't it?" Pastor Pickle said. "Are you here all by yourself?"

"Yeah," replied Kip Kuyper. "I was here with some of my friends, but they all left. I've just been doing some thinking." A small tear trailed down Kip Kuyper's face.

"Oh? About what?" asked Pastor Pickle, as he sat down on the swing next to Kip Kuyper's.

"I'm kind of sad and also kind of mad at some of my friends," said Kip Kuyper, looking down at the ground. "Some of them have been making fun of our school librarian, Mrs. Laila Lateef. She's real nice, but because she always wears that scarf around her head and shoulders, lots of the kids laugh at her and make fun of her behind her back. I don't think that's right."

"You're right, Kip Kuyper!" said Pastor Pickle. "It isn't nice to make fun of anybody, especially just because they may look different than us."

"But you should try telling that to my friends," said Kip Kuyper as he looked up at Pastor Pickle.

"I'd be happy to," smiled Pastor Pickle. "Will you be playing here every day now that school is out for spring break? How about if I meet you and your friends here tomorrow morning? Maybe I can share some thoughts that will help them better understand Mrs. Laila Lateef and anyone else who seems different to them."

"That would be great!" said Kip Kuyper, as he sprang from the swing, patted Doogie on the head and took off down the path toward home.

**The next morning**, when Pastor Pickle and Doogie approached the playground, Kip Kuyper and several of his friends stopped playing and gathered around Pastor Pickle.

"Hey, everybody," said Kip Kuyper. "This is Pastor Pickle. I asked him to meet us here this morning to talk about something important. I've got to be honest with you, I've been feeling bad about how some of us make fun of our librarian because of the way she dresses."

Kip Kuyper stepped back and let Pastor Pickle and Doogie stand in the middle of the circle the kids had formed.

"Thanks, Kip Kuyper," said Pastor Pickle. "I know some of you, but some I don't. So how about if we start by going around the circle and everyone tell me your name?"

"Okay, I'm Kip Kuyper,"
said Kip Kuyper.
"But I guess you
already knew that."
Everyone laughed.

"And I'm
Artie Achesen,"
said the
next boy.

"My name is
Gracie Grandgeorge,"
said the little girl
with the big blue
ribbon in her hair.

"Hi, I'm
Rudy Rivas."

"Hello,
my name is
Haley Han."

"And I'm
Mikey Marble."

"My name is
Tyla Tweeg."

"And this is Doogie," Pastor Pickle said, smiling and pointing at Doogie, who stood with his tail wagging excitedly.

Everyone sat down in a circle in the grass around Pastor Pickle. Doogie stretched out in his favorite shaded spot under the merry-go-round and closed his eyes for a nap.

"I've been hearing that some of your friends have been making fun of people at school who seem to be different from them," began Pastor Pickle. "I'm sure none of you would do that, but I'd like to tell you why it's important that we all be more accepting of everyone around us. Even those who look different for one reason or another.

"Differences are not something to be looked down upon. According to the Bible, they're something we should value and appreciate. Our differences are what add variety and interest to our lives. And you know what? Even though we're all different, God loves each of us just the same. And that's what he wants us to do... love one another."

"Do me a favor and take a minute to look at the person sitting on your right." All the kids looked to their right.

"Now look at the person sitting on your left."

"Did you notice anything about those sitting next to you?" asked Pastor Pickle.

"Yeah," said Mikey Marble. "I noticed Artie Acheson has his shirt on inside out!" Everyone laughed as Artie Acheson's face turned cherry red.

"Did anybody notice anything else?" asked Pastor Pickle. The kids looked around in silence. "Did you notice that neither of the kids sitting beside you look just like you? Kip Kuyper has brown hair and big blue eyes. Artie Achesen has curly red hair, while Gracie Grandgeorge has long brown hair with a big blue bow. Mikey Marble wears glasses and has blond hair and Rudy Rivas has very tanned skin and lots of freckles. Haley Han has beautiful almond-shaped eyes and yellow ribbons in her dark hair. Tyla Tweeg has brown skin and wears her hair in a bun. So, no two of you look anything alike. Can you see that?"

The kids all looked at each other, nodding and smiling.

"So if you think you're all the same, you're wrong," said Pastor Pickle. "We're *all* different. There are more than seven billion people in this world, all individually created by God, and none exactly alike. He did that on purpose! And if God values our differences, shouldn't we do the same?"

"But what about people from other countries?" asked Gracie Grandgeorge. "They're different, aren't they?"

"Let me ask you this," said Pastor Pickle. "What street do you live on, Gracie Grandgeorge?"

"I live on Gibbin Grove," Gracie Grandgeorge replied.

"And what street do you live on, Tyla Tweeg?" Pastor Pickle asked.

"I live on Tumblewood Terrace," answered Tyla Tweeg.

"So you're from different streets. But does that make you different?" asked Pastor Pickle.

"No, people say we're like twins," said Tyla Tweeg with a smile. "We're best friends!"

"Then why would being from a different country be any different than being from a different street?" Pastor Pickle asked.

The kids all looked around the circle at each other.

"I think I can help you see better what I'm trying to say if we all try an experiment. I'm going to give you each this page to color." Pastor Pickle handed each of them a large sheet of paper that had a scene from Pioneer Park outlined in black. Then he gave each of them a blue crayon.

"Please take this page and your crayon home with you and color it tonight."

"But we only have one crayon!" exclaimed Rudy Rivas. "How can we color these trees and flowers and rocks and things if we only have a blue crayon?"

"Just do the best you can," said Pastor Pickle. "And don't cheat. Use only the blue crayon I gave you. Then bring your colored page back here tomorrow and we'll see how you did."

Then Pastor Pickle said a short prayer:

*Dear God,*
*Please be with us as we seek to discover how to love each*
*other unconditionally the way you do. Grant us patience,*
*understanding and grace when we interact with those*
*we think are different from us. Teach us to embrace our*
*differences and realize the joy and blessings they bring to*
*our lives. We earnestly pray these things in the name of*
*your son, Jesus. Amen.*

As they all got up to leave, Artie Acheson looked up at Pastor Pickle and said with a smile, "This is going to be interesting."

**On Tuesday morning**, all the kids were looking at each other's coloring page and giggling when Pastor Pickle and Doogie walked up to meet them.

"So," said Pastor Pickle with a grin. "How did you all do? Did you have fun coloring the page?"

"Not really," said Kip Kuyper, holding up his page for everyone to see. "Actually, it was kind of boring only having a blue crayon."

All the other kids agreed.

Pastor Pickle collected the coloring pages and taped each of them to a bench beside the playground.

Stepping back from them, he said, "Oh. I see what you mean. They all kind of look the same, don't they?

"Yeah," said Haley Han. "They're all just kind of... BLUE!"

"Not very interesting," added Rudy Rivas.

"And not very real," said Mikey Marble.

"Who's ever heard of blue rocks and blue trees?" asked Tyla Tweeg.

"Well, I think that illustrates the point I was trying to make yesterday," continued Pastor Pickle. "Imagine what a boring world we would live in if everybody and everything were just the same, if everything was just… BLUE!"
The kids all nodded.

"I don't know about you," said Pastor Pickle, "but I'm glad God valued differences so much. Things are a lot more interesting when we're not all the same, wouldn't you agree?"

"I sure do now," said Mikey Marble. "I don't think Doogie would like being blue!"

Pastor Pickle and all the kids laughed, and Doogie looked up and wagged his tail when he heard his name.

"I have another assignment for you," Pastor Pickle said, looking around at the kids. "Sometime tonight, please have a conversation with your parents and find out where your family is from."

"But we all live here in Happy Hollow," said Kip Kuyper with a puzzled look on his face.

"I mean ask them where your ancestors are from," said Pastor Pickle. "I think it may surprise you to learn that everyone now living in Happy Hollow came here originally from some other country."

**On Wednesday**, when they all gathered again, Pastor Pickle asked Kip Kuyper what he had found out about his family history.

"I found out my family originally came to America from Holland a long time ago," Kip Kuyper said. "My great-great-grandfather came to find work when he was a teenager. He only spoke Dutch, but soon learned enough English to get by. Over the years my family grew and now we're spread all over the United States. But my dad says we've never forgotten our Dutch heritage."

"And I hope you never do," said Pastor Pickle. "Did you know that at least four of our past presidents had Dutch roots?"

Martin
Van Buren

Theodore
Roosevelt

Warren G.
Harding

Franklin
Roosevelt

"My dad says that Dutch men are, on average, the tallest in the world," said Kip Kuyper proudly.

"Then what happened to you?" Mikey Marble asked, and they all laughed.

"Give him time," said Pastor Pickle. "He isn't finished growing yet. The point is that the customs and traditions the early settlers brought from Holland made our country that much more interesting," continued Pastor Pickle. "Remember, we all bring something different to the group. That's what the word 'diversity' means... our differences. And they should be treasured and celebrated."

Then, Pastor Pickle passed out another coloring sheet of the same scene of the park to all the kids, and gave them each another crayon. But this time it was yellow.

"Please take these home and color them tonight," Pastor Pickle said. "Only this time, you may use your blue crayon and the yellow crayon I just gave you. But only those two."

Then Pastor Pickle asked everyone to stand and he said a short prayer before everyone headed for home.

**The next morning**, when Pastor Pickle got to the playground, the kids already had their latest coloring pages taped to the bench and were gathered around talking about them.

"Good morning!" said Pastor Pickle. "I see you're way ahead of me this morning."

"We couldn't wait to see how everybody colored their homework," said Rudy Rivas. "I've still got a lot of blue rocks but at least my grass is now yellow. It's better than everything being all blue."

"I see someone figured out that if you blend blue and yellow, you get green," said Pastor Pickle, pointing at one of the sheets.

"That's mine," said Haley Han. "I do a lot of coloring and I'm always blending colors to make other colors. It's fun and makes the picture a lot prettier."

"Good for you!" said Pastor Pickle, smiling at Haley Han. "See what happens when you take two completely different things and blend them together? You have blue and yellow, and together they make green... all beautiful colors."

"Haley, did you ask your parents about your family origins?" Pastor Pickle questioned.

"Yes," Haley replied, "and it was exciting to hear the details. I found out my ancestors came to America from China many years ago. My great-great-grandfather, Hye Han, helped build the first railroad across the United States. He met my grandmother on a ranch in Utah where she was a cook."

Rudy Rivas raised his hand, stood, and put on a big, round, broad-brimmed hat with a pointed crown and a colorful band around it.

"My parents told me that my family originally came to America from a small farming area in central Mexico," he said. "This hat is called a *'sombrero'* and my great-grandfather wore it to protect himself from the hot sun while he was working in the field. Here, try it on," said Rudy Rivas, taking the sombrero off his head and handing it to Pastor Pickle.

All the kids laughed when Pastor Pickle put it on. Doogie looked up at Pastor Pickle and barked at him several times.

"My dad said my great-grandparents worked hard in Mexico, mostly raising avocados. To this day, my dad and my grandpa both spread avocado on their toast in the morning instead of butter."

"That sounds good!" said Pastor Pickle. "I might have to give it a try myself."

Pastor Pickle then passed out fresh coloring sheets to the kids.

"Here we go again," said Tyla Tweeg with a chuckle.

"Yep," said Pastor Pickle, as he also gave each of them a new red crayon. "Take this home and color it tonight. Use all three of the crayons I've given you, but only those three. Do the best you can and we'll take a look at them in the morning."

**On Friday**, Pastor Pickle and Doogie joined the kids at the bench in Pioneer Park, where they were examining their coloring sheets and talking among themselves.

"Good morning everybody," said Pastor Pickle, as Doogie headed straight to his favorite spot in the shade under the merry-go-round. "It looks like those colors individually and blended together made a lot of difference in your pictures."

"It sure did!" said Gracie Grandgeorge excitedly. "I finally have a blue sky and green grass. Plus, when I mixed blue and red, I got purple and when I mixed yellow and red, I got orange! It's actually starting to look pretty!"

"So you think having all those different colors makes your park scene look better than when it was only blue?" asked Pastor Pickle.

The kids looked around at each other, shouted, "*YES!*" and gave each other high-fives.

"Well, now you can start to understand why God thinks that all of us being different is way better than all of us being the same, can't you?" said Pastor Pickle. "The different colors and what you can do with them make your pictures a lot more realistic and fun. Think how boring it would be if we all looked, acted, sounded, and thought the same!"

"BORING!" they all shouted at once.

"Artie Achesen," said Pastor Pickle, "what did you find out about where your family is from?"

"Well, I found out my great-great-grandfather came here from Scotland a long time ago on a big ship like the Mayflower," said Artie Achesen.

He took an old photograph out of his pocket and passed it around.

"This is him when he was young, back in Scotland."

"Is he wearing a skirt?" laughed Tyla Tweeg.

"In Scotland, it's called a kilt," answered Artie Achesen. "Lots of men wore them back then. Even today, here in America, some of my relatives wear them on special occasions like family weddings. My dad says it's a way of saying we're proud of our Scottish heritage."

"That's great," smiled Pastor Pickle. "We should all be proud of our family history."

"Mikey Marble, what did you find out about your family's roots?" asked Pastor Pickle.

"I found out my family is originally from Australia," answered Mikey Marble.

Pastor Pickle said, "Did all of you know that the statue of Mayor Milo Marble right here in Pioneer Park is to honor Mikey Marble's great-grandfather, who was Happy Hollow's very first mayor?"

All the kids looked admiringly at Mikey Marble.

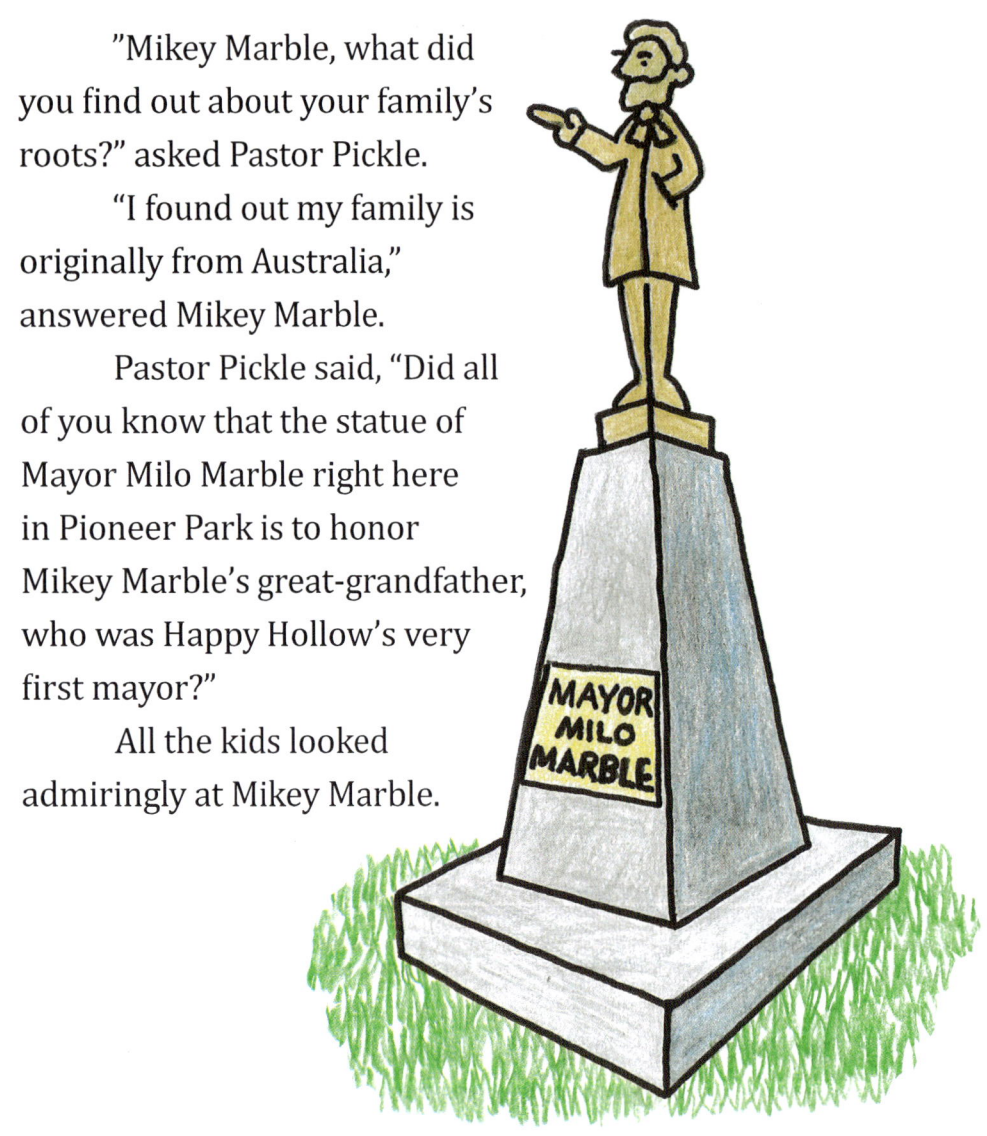

Then, with a smile on his face, Pastor Pickle said, "Guess what?" and began passing out fresh coloring sheets along with a box of eight different colored crayons.

"You know what to do with these," Pastor Pickle said with a grin. Take them home and color them. But this time you can use the full box of crayons. Have fun!"

**The next morning was Saturday** and the kids all had big smiles on their faces when Pastor Pickle and Doogie arrived.

"Why so happy?" asked Pastor Pickle.

"Have you seen our pictures?" asked Haley Han.

"They look so much better now that we have all these colors to work with," said Kip Kuyper. "My sky is blue, my grass is green, my flowers and leaves are colorful and the rocks are finally brown like they're supposed to be!"

"They do look beautiful," said Pastor Pickle, looking at each of their pictures. "And haven't we learned some fun and interesting things about each other this week? You might say that all we've discovered about our families and our differences has added more color and beauty to each of our lives."

"Just like our coloring sheets!" said Gracie Grandgeorge.
"Exactly," Pastor Pickle agreed.

Then Gracie Grandgeorge stood and motioned for Tyla Tweeg to come stand beside her.

"We found out that our families both came here originally from South Africa," said Gracie Grandgeorge.

"I had no idea about that," said Tyla Tweeg. "But now it makes us feel almost like cousins *AND* best friends!"

"So you two have even more in common than you thought," said Pastor Pickle.

"Yes, and my mom gave me this to show everybody," said Gracie Grandgeorge, unfolding a flag that she and Tyla Tweeg held between them. "This is the South African flag and I thought the colors were really pretty!"

"Does everything we've been doing this week make all of you think any differently about people who don't necessarily look, talk or sound the same as you? Does it make you look any differently at people like your librarian, Mrs. Laila Lateef?"

"It sure does," said Mikey Marble. "I'd like to hear her family story too!"

"Well, I have an idea," said Pastor Pickle and he shared his plan with the kids.

**The following Monday**, after school, Pastor Pickle met the kids in the school library, where they told Mrs. Laila Lateef about their diversity project over spring break. She loved what they shared with her. Then Pastor Pickle asked her to tell them all a little bit about her heritage.

"Well, first of all, my parents came to America from Turkey before I was born. Turkey is a Middle Eastern country that has a long and storied history going way back in time. My parents became American citizens and then moved here to Happy Hollow. I was born here, went to school here, and because I've always loved books and learning, after college I became the librarian here at school. My family continued to practice our Muslim faith after coming to America and that's why you always see me wearing this headscarf. It's called a '*HIJAB*' and I wear it as a sign of modesty and respect for my religion. It's very common for Muslim women to wear them, even here in America."

"This past week, the kids have learned the meaning of the word 'diversity' and discovered the richness each of our differences bring to the mix," said Pastor Pickle.

"Mrs. Laila Lateef, Kip Kuyper has something he would like to present to you as a 'thank you' for sharing with us today."

Kip Kuyper handed Mrs. Laila Lateef a framed picture of the scene in Pioneer Park they had all hand-colored with the full box of crayons.

"This is so we will always remember what a beautiful and colorful world we live in when we value and celebrate our many differences," said Pastor Pickle.

With tears in her eyes, Mrs. Laila Lateef thanked each of them. "This means so much to me."

Then Pastor Pickle said, "The world needs to learn this lesson. I say we all agree to share it with others whenever we can."

One by one, they put their hands together in a circle and shouted, "Let's share it!"

And with a huge smile on his face, Pastor Pickle said, "AMEN!"

# A Message From Pastor Pickle

"Diversity" is just a big word that means we're all different. The fact that God didn't make anyone else in the whole world exactly like you or me must mean he loves diversity. And if he does, we should too!

Diversity isn't just about where we live. It's also about how we look, how we act, how we think, and even what we choose to believe. Some of us are young, others are older. Half of us are boys. The other half are girls.

But it's our many differences that make the world so interesting! Remember how boring the coloring page was when everything was just blue? God made many people with a full range of differences, and yet he commands us to love one another, and he means everyone.

    We must respect our differences and celebrate how much color and beauty they add to our lives!

    Say this prayer with me:

**Dear God**

**Thank you for being our creator. Help us see the beauty in everything and everybody you've created. Teach us to see the world through your eyes, embracing the colorful richness every person brings into our lives. Regardless of our differences, remind us to always love each other as you do. With thankful hearts, we pray these things.**

    **Amen**

# Additional References

'Love your neighbor as yourself.' No other commandment is greater than these."
Mark 12:31 (NLT)

In this new life, it doesn't matter if you are a Jew or Gentile, circumcised or uncircumcised, barbaric, uncivilized, slave or free. Christ is all that matters, and he lives in all of us.
Colossians 3:11 (NLT)

For Christ himself has brought peace to us. He united Jews and Gentiles into one people when, in his own body on the cross, he broke down a wall of hostility that separated us.
Ephesians 2:14 (NLT)

Then Peter replied, "I see very clearly that God shows no favoritism. In every nation he accepts those who fear him and do what is right."
Acts 10:34-35 (NLT)

# Additional References *(cont.)*

Yes, the body has many different parts, not just one part. If the foot says, "I am not a part of the body because I am not a hand," that does not make it any less a part of the body. And if the ear says, "I am not part of the body because I am not an eye," would that make it any less a part of the body? If the whole body were an eye, how would we hear? Or if your whole body were an ear, how would you smell anything? But our bodies have many different parts, and God has put each part just where he wants it. How strange a body would be if it had only one part! Yes, there are many parts, but only one body. The eye can never say to the hand, "I don't need you." The head can't say to the feet, "I don't need you."
1 Corinthians 12:14-21 (NLT)

After this I saw a vast crowd, too great to count, from every nation and tribe and people and language, standing in front of the throne and before the Lamb.
Revelation 7:9 (NLT)

## Lessons for Living Series

### Pastor Pickle and the Unique Boy
Recognizing special God-given gifts

### Pastor Pickle and the Let's Go! Club
Physical, spiritual and emotional health

### Pastor Pickle and the Criss-Cross Signal
Responding in love to stressful encounters

### Pastor Pickle and the Bumble Bees
Dealing with conflicting emotions during a divorce

### Pastor Pickle and the Full Box of Crayons
Learning to embrace diversity

Available at
amazon

and select bookstores

97827748R00033

Made in the USA
Columbia, SC
14 June 2018